What in the World?

According to Greek
mythology, Prometheus
was a god who saved the
human race by giving
them a torch from the sun.
The fire, and the light
that it produced, served
as protection.

The Light Bulb

Jennifer Fandel

Creative Education

Introduction

With a surge of electrical current, the delicate, arch-shaped filament began to glow. The simple light did not falter as it radiated from the clear glass bulb. It was steady, its brightness filtering as easily as sunlight over the tables and tools of the workshop. The team of assistants stopped their work, drawn to the light that Thomas Edison held in his hands. Throughout the night, their eyes were transfixed, their faces lit with satisfaction. "The light still burns," Thomas declared, as the light shone through the night to the breaking dawn and beyond. The control of day and night was now in his hands.

Gas lamps were the most common light source before incandescent light bulbs. These lights flickered, and the oil or gas smoked and clouded the glass lamps.

Gas lamps were widely used in Europe and the United States by 1820.

Inventors had been working on an incandescent bulb for almost 60 years by the time Edison perfected it.

Thanks to the need for cheap railroad labor, California was home to about 50,000 Chinese by 1870.

Railroad terminals made towns such as New Orleans, Louisiana, into major cities and centers of commerce.

The Big, Wide World

Thomas Edison began his work on the electric light bulb in New Jersey in the 1870s, a time when the United States and much of the world ached with the growing pains of progress. Across the wide American landscape, homesteaders claimed land, miners panned for silver and gold in the rugged West, and workers pounded spikes along thousands of miles of

From 1852 to 1875, many Chinese people left their country because of droughts and famines. These immigrants played a key role in finishing the transcontinental railroad in the American West.

railway. The desire for movement characterized the nation. Horses and wagons filled the rutted dirt roads of cities and towns. Steamboats chugged up and down the Mississippi River. And with the completion of the transcontinental railroad in 1869, connecting the east and west coasts of America, the rumble and whistle of trains filled the air.

Steam engines built in the mid-1870s would help give rise to the automobile industry.

Italian immigrants bound for the United States; many such immigrants settled in New York.

In the 1860s, the modern nation of Germany was born when a number of previously separate states were united under the powerful state of Prussia and its prime minister, Otto von Bismarck.

In the territories and 38 states of the growing country, people sought better opportunities for themselves and their families. European immigrants populated the East, often crowding into city tenements. Many also settled in the Midwest and Great Plains, living in simple sod or wood structures and farming fresh plots of land. Others worked in logging camps or coal mines. Ex-slaves, newly freed after the Civil War, traveled up from the South to seek work in the North's flourishing steel and textile industries. While many parts of the South struggled to rebuild their war-ravaged cities and towns, the North and West prospered.

Otto von Bismarck

Slavery was halted by the Civil War in 1865.

There were fortunes to be made, and the pursuit of new technologies inspired the work of some of history's brightest minds. The telegraph, created in 1837 by American inventor Samuel Morse, clicked day and night, bridging distances through rapid communication. In 1876, Alexander Graham Bell invented the telephone, which largely replaced the telegraph in short order. Improved steam engines and electric generators, meanwhile, fulfilled the growing demand for power in the industries of the North.

Alexander Graham Bell was 29 years old when he created his telephone, changing communication forever.

Buenos Aires harbor was a primary commercial outlet for South America in the late 1800s.

In remote parts of the Amazon rainforest, ancient hunting and gathering tribes such as the Yanomami and Kayapo remained virtually unknown to the outside world until as late as the 1980s.

In South America during this time, most of the continent was plagued by political instability, poverty, and transportation problems through the mountainous terrain and tropical forests. Argentina, however, entered a "golden age" spurred by foreign trade and the use of new technologies. Cattle ranchers received the latest beef prices on the world markets via the telegraph, and newly invented refrigerated ships transported their fresh beef to Europe. The effects of this booming economy were best seen in Argentina's coastal capital, Buenos Aires, which gained prominence as the "Paris of South America" with its paved streets, lush public gardens, and grand buildings.

The late 1870s saw the birth of two artists who would go on to help define the avant-garde style of painting. Swiss artist Paul Klee and Russian Kazimir Malevich would both earn fame with their experimental styles.

The Impressionist art movement gained momentum in Europe during the 1870s and 1880s. Frenchmen Pierre Auguste Renoir, Edgar Degas, and Claude Monet painted during this time.

A sampling of artwork from Paul Klee (top), Kazimir Malevich (bottom), and Edgar Degas (opposite).

A depiction of a calico printing press, at which dyed fabrics were produced, in 19th-century England.

Across the Atlantic, new machines in such industries as textile and iron production made many skilled English workers obsolete and factory owners rich. The city of London, home to five million people by 1880, exhibited the worst effects of this industrialization. The poor scrounged garbage heaps for food and used dirty rags to keep warm at night. Harsh living conditions and frequent cholera epidemics caused early deaths, and many young orphans were left to beg in the streets. Conversely, life was carefree for royalty and the wealthy, who filled their days with social events while servants prepared their meals and cleaned their mansions.

With the new emphasis on industry in the late 1870s came changes in American food. The Kellogg Company introduced the first breakfast cereal, Granula, and people could buy roasted coffee packed in sealed cans.

This illustration by Italian Roberto Innocenti depicts the despair felt by many English laborers in the late 1800s.

Before European colonists arrived, most Africans lived a self-sufficient existence as farmers. When colonists began populating Africa, many natives began working for European gain, building railroads, mining diamonds, and laboring on rubber, sugar, and cocoa plantations.

Christian missionaries first journeyed into Africa in the early 1800s and stayed for more than a century.

Most Africans in the 1870s lived in farming villages on grasslands or deep inside forested areas. Their homes were made of mud or clay and thatch. Fur rugs, fur blankets, and mats made of river plants called rushes served as furniture.

In 1878, the Tiffany Diamond was found in a South African mine. It was the largest and finest yellow diamond ever discovered.

To the south of England, Britain and France led the so-called "Scramble for Africa." European countries claimed the lands and riches of Africa—including diamonds and gold—as their own and established large farms and coffee plantations, employing natives as their workers. One of the few positive effects of this European invasion was the work of missionaries, whose efforts to spread literacy among the African people (most of whom were farmers or hunters) would eventually improve Africans' lives economically. Similar stories of expansion unfolded in Asia during this time.

Many white missionaries in the 1870s embraced the simple life of the African peoples they educated.

In the days of gas lamps and arc lamps, the German states were among Europe's best-lit countries.

The romanticism of indoor lighting is apparent in The Elegant Soiree, *a painting by Frenchman Victor Gilbert.*

When people first obtained incandescent lights for their homes, many did not cover the bulbs with fixtures or shades. They liked the bright light and enjoyed showing off the invention.

In the late 19th century, the world was changing quickly. Communication was improving, making the world seem smaller. But amid the large-scale industrialization and expansion and widening division between the haves and the have-nots, one man saw beyond the desire for wealth to an essential that humans had been seeking throughout their existence: light. With light—practical, affordable light—he would be placing time and opportunity in people's hands.

Although rather unremarkable in appearance, the incandescent bulb altered human history.

The Wizard of Invention

Thomas Alva Edison was born on February 11, 1847, in Milan, Ohio. The youngest of seven children born to Sam and Nancy Edison, Thomas was known as Al or Alva to the members of his family. The Edisons moved north to Port Huron, Michigan, soon after Thomas's birth.

Thomas's childhood was filled with books and the joys of scientific experimentation.

A sickly child, Edison lost his hearing in one ear after a bout with scarlet fever. His hearing worsened throughout his life.

Attending school sporadically, Thomas received the majority of his primary education under his mother's supervision. He spent hours poring over his favorite book, *The School of Natural Philosophy*, which encouraged him to construct a chemistry lab in his basement. English scientist Michael Faraday's work with electricity was another of Thomas's favorite subjects.

A photograph of Thomas Edison as a young boy.

Two intellectual giants of Edison's formative years: philosopher Karl Marx (left) and author Leo Tolstoy (right).

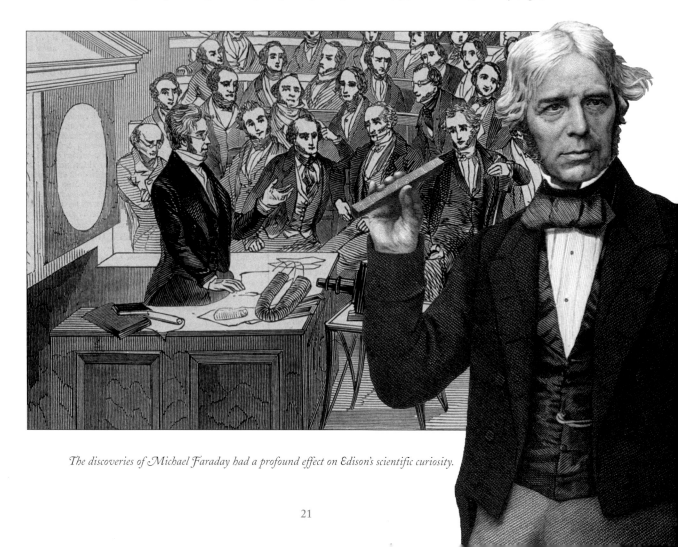

The discoveries of Michael Faraday had a profound effect on Edison's scientific curiosity.

But Thomas had yet another love: the railroad. He was fascinated by the trains that traveled through his town and, like other boys of his time, aspired to be a train engineer. When a job selling newspapers and candy on the trains became available, Thomas took it. At age 12, he worked 12-hour days shuttling back and forth on the Grand Trunk Railroad between Port Huron and Detroit. The railway inspired Thomas's enterprising spirit, and he became a pro at his job, sometimes earning the grand sum of $10 a day. He soon hired a few boys under him, which gave him time for other ventures. He purchased a used printing press for the train and produced a daily newspaper that often served between 250 and 500 subscribers.

At the age of 15, Thomas learned how to operate a telegraph, a skill that connected him to a world beyond his train route. Once the dots and dashes became a familiar language to him, he struck out on his own. Between the ages of 16 and 20, Thomas rode trains from telegraph office to telegraph office, eventually making it to the East Coast.

Edison liked playing jokes on people. As a young telegrapher, he would often attach batteries to objects such as communal wash tanks so that people would get a shock. Many co-workers tired of this prank, but Edison never did.

Edison slept only four to five hours a night. Many times he would simply clear a desk or worktable when he felt tired and sleep there.

Edison was drawn to the bustle and enterprise of railroad depots, such as this one in Durand, Michigan.

Beginning in 1868 under teen-aged emperor Mutsuhito, Japan spent the late 1800s building itself into a military and economic power, developing a national military, education system, railway, and newspapers fashioned after European models.

Edison sent his assistants around the world to find the perfect filament. For 14 years, a specific type of bamboo found only adjacent to a Shinto shrine in Kyoto, Japan, was used for the filament material.

In the 1860s and 1870s, Japan adopted a Western-influenced military system (top) and railway systems (bottom).

During his years as a telegrapher, Thomas became increasingly frustrated by the slowness of the telegraph, which transmitted only one message at a time. After years of experimenting on the job, he invented a number of improved telegraphs, each model able to transmit more and more messages. After this success, Thomas quit telegraphy to become a full-time inventor. It was a bold move, even in a time of rapid innovation and enterprise, but confidence was something that the 22-year-old had in ample supply.

A photograph of Edison as a young man (top), around the time he turned from telegrapher to inventor.

Edison fishing with one of his sons (top left);

his first wife, Mary (top right and

bottom right); Edison with his

second wife, Mina (left).

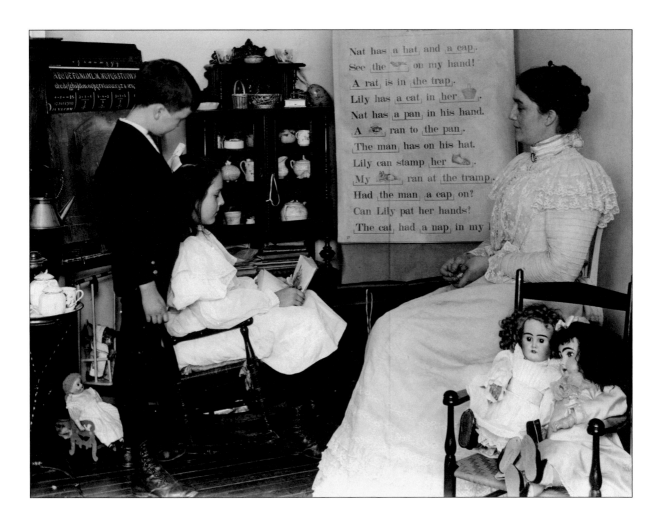

When Edison courted his second wife, Mina, he taught her Morse code so that he could court her "in private" while in the company of other people. He proposed to her using Morse code.

Soon after Thomas struck out on his own, he met his future wife, a 16-year-old telegraph operator named Mary Stillwell. They married on Christmas Day in 1871 and had three children. Their 13-year marriage was a troubled one, as Mary struggled with various illnesses and anger at her often-distant and always-working husband. Mary would die in 1884, and Thomas would remarry. His second wife, Mina Miller, was a well-educated woman from a prominent family, and together they too would have three children.

By many accounts, Edison was a distant husband and father, leaving care of his children to his wives.

In 1876, five years after wedding Mary, Thomas moved his young family to Menlo Park, New Jersey. Menlo Park was located in the country, little more than a whistle-stop outside of the bustling eastern cities, and there Thomas set up an invention business with a staff of 12 assistants. When Thomas stated that he expected to make "a minor invention every ten days and a big thing every six months or so," the newspapers dubbed him the "Wizard of Menlo Park."

Edison's early scientific facilities (top), and his spacious facilities at Menlo Park (bottom and opposite).

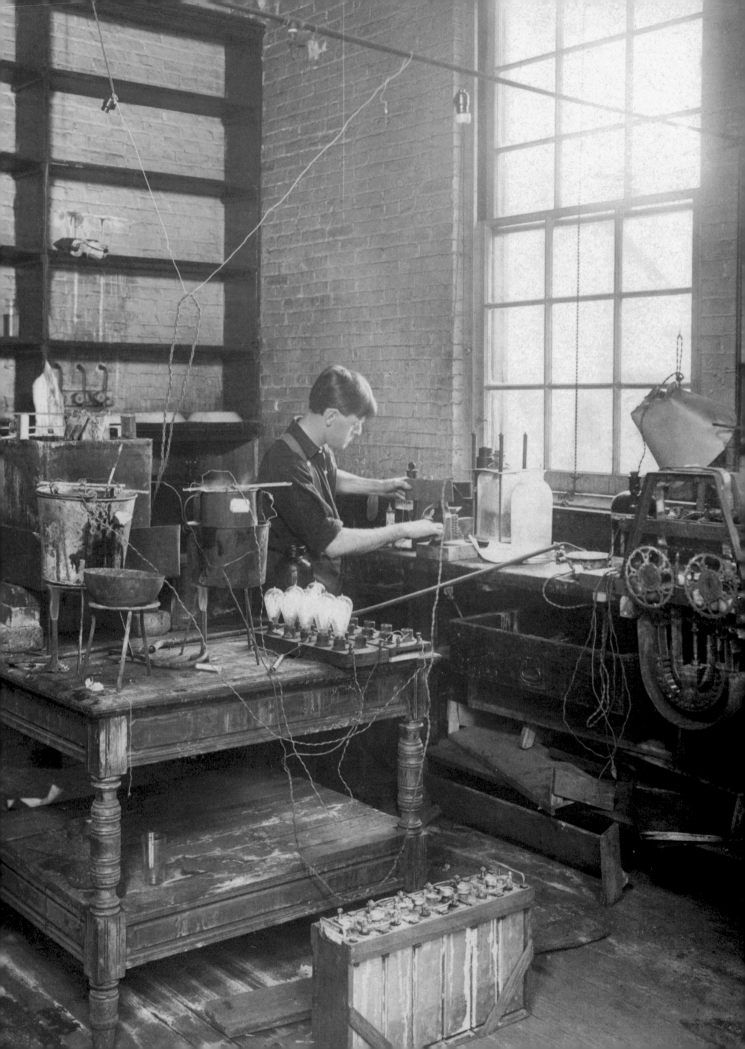

The early days of Thomas's "invention factory" produced astonishing success. In 1877, Thomas and his staff introduced the carbon transmitter, which improved early telephone technology. Also in 1877, Thomas invented the phonograph, the first instrument to play recorded sound. Thomas was surprised by the immediate attention that he received for an invention that he thought quite fanciful.

When Edison founded his invention factory in Menlo Park, it included an office, lab, and machine shop. He later added more assistants to staff a glass-blowing house, photography studio, carpenter's shop, carbon production shed, blacksmith shop, and library.

The first words Edison uttered into his original phonograph in 1877 were "Mary had a little lamb."

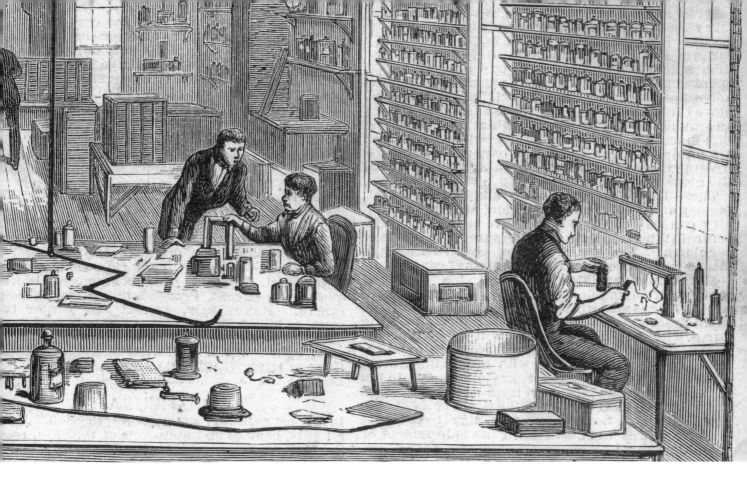

Edison left notebooks on worktables throughout his laboratory so that he and his assistants could record ideas, make sketches, and note the outcome of experiments. He filled 3,400 notebooks in his lifetime.

The newspapers delighted in delivering the latest news from Menlo Park. Most indulged their readers with details that made Thomas seem a curious mix of wizard and common man, with more than a touch of boyishness. He could often be found in the center of the action in the lab, besmirched with dirt and grease, his clothes rumpled, and his hair uncombed. And his uncompromising stare told onlookers that he didn't care how he looked. He had more important things on his mind, things that pushed him to work late into the night and kept him from sleep, his home, and his family. He was driven by the pursuit of light.

Edison's lab was designed to give his assistants room and freedom in their pursuit of practical inventions.

From the earliest times, people have always associated light with warmth and security.

The Quest for Light

For the earliest humans, darkness often equaled fear and evil; for without light, one could not see the dangers that lurked after nightfall. The need for protection and safety encouraged humans to develop increasingly better methods for keeping light. They first used torches, then candles, then gas-powered lamps. Nevertheless, a major problem continued to exist. Light meant the flames of fire, and fire was fickle and dangerous. It was not until Thomas's work that the dream of making light without fire became reality.

This was no easy task. Throughout the 1800s, many scientists and inventors tried their hands at making electric light. The arc lamp was the first major lighting development. Well developed by the 1870s, it proved unsuitable for indoor lighting because of its harsh brightness and was practical only outdoors. Still, people loved the new light, promenading the city streets at night, and their favorable reactions encouraged a handful of inventors to struggle with the intricacies of incandescent light.

Despite their limitations, arc lamps revolutionized outdoor lighting, as here in Minneapolis, Minnesota.

The word "incandescent" comes from a Latin word that means "to glow with heat." The incandescent light bulb, as developed in the 1870s, used a fairly low electric current from a dynamo, or electric generator, to heat a filament to a point at which it glowed. This light was brighter than candles and lamps, but it was not harsh on the eyes. As Thomas worked on incandescent light, he dreamed of its convenience. By being able to light up the night with the flip of

The famous quotation "Genius is 1 percent inspiration and 99 percent perspiration" was coined by Edison. It was quoted in *Harper's Monthly* in 1932.

Edison's attempts to perfect the incandescent bulb were powered by a dynamo like the one shown above.

a switch, businesses could work around the clock. No longer would night dictate the schedules of human activity.

Thomas's vision of his new invention seemed so simple, but his work on it stretched more than a year. When one part of his light bulb seemed perfected, another part went awry. The only thing that remained constant was the glass bulb, which had been designed by a German artisan newly hired by Thomas. The first bulbs were hand-blown into perfectly round globes of clear glass. Narrowed to a slim base, each bulb was accented by a small curl of glass at the top of the globe. The curl of glass was produced as air was exhausted from the bulb and the bulb was sealed.

Edison's original light bulb was basic in its structure but required precise glass work and construction.

The gas lamps burned night after night as Thomas conducted well over 1,000 light bulb experiments. He consistently ran into two related problems: vacuum pumps that were too weak to exhaust enough oxygen from the bulbs, and, consequently, filaments that burned out too soon. After reading about British inventor Joseph Swan's experiments with carbon paper filaments, Thomas tried them, but the light burned out within minutes. During his search for filaments—which included everything from human hair and platinum to bamboo and coconut fiber—a better vacuum pump was developed for the removal of oxygen. Thomas's moment of triumph was finally at hand.

Joseph Swan, whose contributions to the light bulb and other inventions earned him British knighthood in 1904.

It was 1879, on a night like many nights at Menlo Park. After months of frustration with inadequate filaments, Thomas rolled some of his wife's sewing thread in carbon dust. He bent the thread into an arch and inserted it into the bulb. Then he exhausted the air and attached the bulb's electric wires to a dynamo. As his staff looked on, Thomas raised the voltage levels, and the bulb began to glow. For more than 13 hours, the bulb brightened the room. Thomas knew that the first part of his quest was over.

Edison sees the fruits of his labor in this illustration of the first successful bulb lighting in 1879.

Edison has been immortalized in many works of art, such as this illustration by American Dean Cornwell.

The Sarah Jordan boardinghouse, which was located down the street from Menlo Park, was the first home to be lit with Edison light.

On the night of December 31, 1879, people came to Menlo Park to see what they could not imagine. Trainloads of people rushed off the passenger cars and drew breath at the magnificent sight. A trail of resplendent light shone from light poles between the train station and the lab and buildings of Thomas's invention factory. The snow fairly shone, and the windows of the buildings glowed with the steadiest light. The Wizard of Menlo Park had indeed captured daylight and placed it within delicate bulbs of glass.

An artistic rendering of Edison's famous invention factory compound in Menlo Park.

Edison never succumbed to the idea of being rich, even though he was a millionaire by the age of 40. He once said, "I don't care so much for fortune as I do for getting ahead of the other fellows."

Edison built a small electric railroad around Menlo Park. His assistants often rode it to their favorite fishing hole nearby. This was a prototype of early trolleys and subway systems.

But Thomas had no intention of stopping there. To make the invention so affordable that, as Thomas said, "only the rich would dine by candlelight," he envisioned an entire electrical system to power his lights. Thomas and his team built a large electrical generator at the Pearl Street Station in New York City, and soon the city replaced its underground gas lines with electric lines. By 1882, the Pearl Street Station generated electricity for the financial district of New York, lighting the prominent offices of Wall Street. From that day onward, there was no looking back. Electric light spread throughout the nation and the world, and the power of light was put into the hands of the common man.

The development of the light bulb was largely paralleled by that of skyscrapers and small rail systems.

French chemist Marie Curie earned fame with her work on radioactivity at the turn of the 20th century.

An improvement in organization and more visible tactics such as boycotts and picketing earned American and English women voting rights by the 1920s.

The suffragist movement, seeking women's voting rights, peaked in the late 1800s and early 1900s.

Thomas Edison is today widely regarded as history's most prolific inventor, having earned patents for 1,093 inventions during his lifetime. But none of his inventions is as revered as the incandescent light bulb. On the day of Thomas's funeral, on October 21, 1931, people across the United States honored him by turning out their lights. For one minute, darkness graced the nation. And then, one by one, the lights came back on.

Edison in his laboratory later in life (above); a German light bulb advertisement from the early 1900s (opposite).

ALLGEMEINE ELEKTRICITÆTS GESELLSCHAFT

A·E·G·METALLFADENLAMPE

ZIRKA EIN WATT PRO KERZE

What in the World?

By 1885, the bicycle had assumed roughly the size and form in which it exists today.

German Karl Benz (above, at right) followed Edison as a newsmaker with his 1880s work on the automobile.

1847	Thomas Alva Edison is born in Milan, Ohio.
1850	Levis blue jeans are introduced by Levi Strauss in San Francisco, California.
1850–1860	More than two million immigrants come to the United States from Europe.
1855	The Louvre, a magnificent art gallery, opens in Paris, France.
1861–1865	The Union and the Confederacy fight in the United States Civil War.
1866	Swedish engineer Alfred Nobel invents dynamite.
1869	The Suez Canal through Egypt is completed, opening Asia to further European trade and colonization.
1876	Edison moves into his Menlo Park lab.
1879	Edison unveils his incandescent light bulb to the public.
1885	The world's first skyscraper, a 10-story building in Chicago, Illinois, is completed.
1889	Electric lighting is installed in the White House.
1891	The game of basketball is invented in Massachusetts.
1892	Russian composer Petr Ilich Tchaikovsky writes *The Nutcracker Suite*, a musical ballet.
1900	Escape artist and magician Harry Houdini escapes from London's Scotland Yard in a legendary stunt.
1911–1920	The Mexican Revolution occurs. It is the first effort in Latin America to empower the poor.
1914	William Wrigley Jr. invents Doublemint chewing gum.
1914–1918	World War I is fought in Europe. About 10 million people die in the conflict.
1928	Walt Disney draws the first "Mickey Mouse" cartoon.
1929	The stock market crashes, starting the Great Depression in America.
1931	Edison dies at the age of 84.

Copyright

Published by Creative Education
123 South Broad Street, Mankato, Minnesota 56001

Creative Education is an imprint of The Creative Company.
Design by Rita Marshall
Production design by Kathleen Petelinsek

Photographs by: Art Resource (Digital image © The Museum of
Modern Art/Licensed by SCALA, The New York Public Library,
CNAC/MNAM/Dist. Réunion des Musées Nationaux), Corbis
(Archivo Iconografico; S.A., Bettmann, Christie's Images, Christel
Gerstenberg, Hulton-Deutsch Collection, Minnesota Historical Society,
Gianni Dagli Orti, Schenectady Museum; Hall of Electrical History
Foundation, Leonard de Selva, Swim Ink, Underwood & Underwood),
Historypictures.com, Krefelder Kunstmuseen/ Kaiser Wilhelm Museum

Illustrations: copyright © 2005 Jean-Louis Besson (4, 5, 41), © 2005
Etienne Delessert (37), © 2005 Roberto Innocenti (15, 32), © 2005
John Thompson (9)

Library of Congress Cataloging-in-Publication Data
Fandel, Jennifer.
The light bulb / by Jennifer Fandel.
p. cm. — (What in the world?)
Summary: Describes the work of the inventor Thomas Alva Edison
in creating the incandescent light bulb.
ISBN 1-58341-271-9
1. Light bulbs—Juvenile literature. [1. Light bulbs. 2. Edison,
Thomas A. (Thomas Alva), 1847-1931. 3. Inventors.] I. Title. II. Series.

TK4351.F36 2003   621.32'6—dc21   2003046284

First Edition
9 8 7 6 5 4 3 2 1

Index